THE WORLD OF THE
COYOTE

THE WORLD OF THE
COYOTE

WAYNE GRADY

SIERRA CLUB BOOKS

SAN FRANCISCO

The Sierra Club, founded in 1892 by John Muir, has devoted itself to the study and protection of the Earth's scenic and ecological resources—mountains, wetlands, woodlands, wild shores and rivers, deserts and plains. The publishing program of the Sierra Club offers books to the public as a nonprofit educational service in the hope that they may enlarge the public's understanding of the Club's basic concerns. The point of view expressed in each book, however, does not necessarily represent that of the Club. The Sierra Club has some sixty chapters coast to coast, in Canada, Hawaii, and Alaska. For information about how you may participate in its programs to preserve wilderness and the quality of life, please address inquiries to Sierra Club, 730 Polk Street, San Francisco, CA 94109.

Sierra Club Books paperback edition: 1995

Originally published in Canada by Greystone Books, a division of Douglas & McIntyre Ltd., 1615 Venables Street, Vancouver, British Columbia V5L 2H1

LIBRARY OF CONGRESS CATALOGING IN PUBLICATION DATA

Grady, Wayne, 1948–
        The world of the coyote / Wayne Grady.
            p.   cm.
        Includes bibliographical references (p.   ) and index.
        ISBN 0-87156-376-2
        1. Coyotes.   I. Title.
        QL737.C22G625 1994
        599.74'442—dc20   94-1464
                                                     CIP

Cover design by Barbara Hodgson
Book design by Barbara Hodgson
Edited by Nancy Flight
Maps by Fiona MacGregor
Printed and bound in Hong Kong

10 9 8 7 6 5 4 3 2 1

Pages 2–3: Photograph by Tim Fitzharris
Pages 8–9: Photograph by Leonard Lee Rue III

CONTENTS

ACKNOWLEDGEMENTS

Among the many people who have helped me during the research and writing of this book, I particularly want to thank Mike Gibeau, Colleen Campbell and Paul Paquet, who are conducting valuable wild canine studies in Banff National Park, Alberta. I also want to thank Bob Crabtree, of Bozeman, Montana, for taking time out of a harried week to patiently answer my questions, and Kezha Hatier, for letting me tag along with her in Yellowstone National Park, Wyoming. In addition, Mike Gibeau and Bob Crabtree reviewed the first draft of this book and made many helpful suggestions. Others who have helped greatly include Arlen Todd, Dennis Voigt, Mike Buss, Maria Delmeida, Dean Cluff and Arnold Boer.

I am also grateful to Candace Savage for her wise counsel and warm hospitality during the book's formative stages. To Nancy Flight, whose editorial advice has been much appreciated and often followed. To Reg Martin, Pam Green, Kenneth de Kok and Carolyn Smart for their friendship and support. And, throughout this project as for so many others, to Merilyn Simonds Mohr, the reader over my shoulder.

FACING PAGE: RICK McINTYRE

INTRODUCTION

I'm the voice of all the Wildest West, the Patti of the Plains;
I'm a wild Wagnerian opera of diabolic strains;
I'm a roaring, ranting orchestra with lunatics becrammed;
I'm a vocalized tornado—I'm the shrieking of the damned.

—Ernest Thompson Seton, "The Coyote's Song," 1913

The first time I heard coyotes howling was on a cold, clear night in late October in eastern Ontario. I had just stepped outside to look up at the stars when I heard a sudden ghostlike chorus of rising and falling ululations coming from the other side of a granite ridge that cuts across a muskrat swamp to the south of the cabin. I listened for nearly half an hour, caught by the haunting melody, fascinated by what was obviously not just a random series of howls but parts of a conversation. The sounds seemed to tremble on the verge of language, to be, almost literally, the voice of the wilderness.

I have since learned that coyotes howl for a number of reasons, most of which are understood only by coyotes. "They are the most vocal of all North American wild mammals," writes H. T. Gier, a wildlife biologist at the University of Kansas, "but unfortunately, coyote communications have not been analyzed." Like wolves and birds, members of a coyote pack vocalize to keep in touch with one another, as well as for other reasons. The scientific name for the coyote, *Canis latrans*, means "barking dog," and the epithet is well deserved: wolves rarely bark, and foxes rarely talk outside of mating season, but a short, sharp yip from a

FACING PAGE: *A coyote pounces on its tiny prey. Coyotes differ from wolves in that they hunt alone and up to 80 per cent of their diet consists of rodents.* JEFF FOOTT

mother coyote will send her pups scurrying for cover, a slightly modified vocalization will bring them running for dinner, and other calls seem to indicate fear, pain, pleasure, curiosity and, as Gier adds, "probably some deeper feelings and needs of the caller."

These calls also seem to express some deeper feelings and needs of the listener. Especially since the near-extirpation of the grey wolf from our forests, the call of the coyote has become the call of the wild, at least as much so as the bugling of elk or the honking of Canada geese. "For my family," Nora M. Stewart wrote in an article in *Blue Jay* magazine, "a recent northern holiday was made more memorable when coyotes seemed to ring our campsite and provide a lively serenade in stereo." Stewart, writing in 1972—the year the use of poisons to kill coyotes was finally banned on public land in the United States by President Richard Nixon—was lamenting the loss of that lively serenade in many parts of southern Canada. Her article—"Coyote Management in Saskatchewan: Is Poison the Answer?"—is a reflection of the concern many of us have felt about the wanton destruction of the coyote wherever it intersects with human activity. Stewart quotes Ernest Thompson Seton, the nineteenth-century naturalist and author of *Wild Animals I Have Known*: "If ever the day should come when one may camp in the West, and hear not a note of the coyote's joyous stirring evening song," Seton wrote, "I hope that I shall long before have passed away, gone over the Great Divide." Seton went over the Great Divide in 1946, by which time the coyote's song had been all but silenced in many parts of its historical range.

My own interest in coyotes began a few years ago, when I was accompanying Paul Rezendes, a professional tracker in Massachussets, to look for evidence of coyote predation on deer in the Quabbin Reserve, a huge wildlife refuge surrounding an artificial reservoir that supplies the city of Boston with drinking water. We didn't see any coyotes—coyotes are not an endangered species by any means, but they are rarely seen in the woods unless they want to be, and that day they didn't want to be—but we found plenty of coyote and deer sign, in the form of tracks, scat, day beds, browse and scrapes, to suggest that both species were alive and well in the area. As we walked, Paul talked about his encounters with the eastern coyote, about watching from a shallow ravine as a male coyote squared off against a female white-tailed deer who had broken her hind leg in the deep snow and, later, about watching as the entire pack fed off the kill, the alpha pair first, then the younger animals, in an almost ritualistically prescribed pecking order. He referred to coyotes as "ghosts of the forest" and said they instilled in him a deep sense that nature is not something "out there, apart and remote from us," but that we are all part of nature. "What happens in the forest," he said, "happens to us."

Although coyote sign—from footprints in the snow along a remote forest trail to the remains of a meal on an urban "nature path"—can be found almost anywhere if one knows how to recognize it, most people hear many more coyotes than they see: coyotes are crepuscular hunters, for one thing, preferring to do most of their foraging in the late evening, as well as the early morning, when it is to their advantage to remain unseen. And they have become understandably wary of being seen by humans. Some old-time coyote hunters say they have never seen a coyote broadside. But with patience, a good pair of binoculars and one of the many wildlife biologists who make it their business to study coyotes in their natural surroundings, in the past year or so I have seen coyotes in many different kinds of habitat—in the boreal forests of Ontario, in the mountains of Alberta and Wyoming, on the rolling Saskatchewan prairie and on the arid plateaus of South Dakota. I have watched them hunting Uinta ground squirrels in Yellowstone National Park; I have looked for their den sites in Banff; I have watched a female sitting patiently on the shoulder of a road, keeping vigil beside the body of her mate. They are exquisitely beautiful animals, with rich, multicoloured coats, feline movements, a sharp intelligence in their eyes. They seem to me to combine the sleekness of the cat, the quick intelligence of the fox and the brute wildness of the wolf. They also seem to survive, against all odds, with the tenacity of life itself.

One day last summer, I was hiking along a back-country trail in Yellowstone National Park and stopped to eat lunch at the top of a high mountain ridge that looked out over a lush, green valley. As I sat down on a rock at the edge of the cliff, my foot jangled a length of chain that disappeared into a small crevice. When I dug the debris out of the crevice, I discovered that the chain was attached to an ancient, rusted leg-hold trap that had evidently lain there undisturbed since the late 1930s, when trapping coyotes was banned in the park. Like that trap, our attitudes towards coyotes have lingered on long after legislation and science have come to the coyote's defence. We have tried our damnedest to exterminate the coyote, and many of us continue to try our damnedest today. Fortunately, we have not succeeded. This book is an attempt to understand what the coyote is and why we have been so determined to eradicate it; it is also a celebration of our lack of success.

PART 1

COYOTES & NATURE

Coyotes often seek out high vantage points from which to scout out the surrounding territory. ESTHER SCHMIDT/VALAN PHOTOS

COYOTES & NATURE

*Gliding about in their shady forest homes, keeping
well out of sight, there is a multitude of sleek
clad animals living and enjoying their clean,
beautiful lives. How beautiful and interesting they are
is about as difficult for busy mortals to find out
as if their homes were beyond sight in the sky.*

—John Muir, "The Forests of Oregon," 1880

FIRST ENCOUNTERS

On a warm afternoon in late July, as I was driving along a narrow, winding road in Banff
National Park, Alberta, I interrupted the progress of a mother coyote and three pups as they
were crossing from a steep, pine-covered slope on the right to a low meadow on the left.
The female and two of the pups had made it safely across, but my approach had stranded
the third pup halfway up the slope on the right. When I pulled over to the side of the road,
I could see him through the lodgepole pines, wanting to continue, hesitating, starting forward again, then backing up. He reminded me of an over-eager base runner waiting for the
sign to steal second.

Down among the wolf willows, Mama simply sat down with her two young ones to wait
for me to leave. As she waited, the two pups gamboled beside her, rolling over each other,
chewing at each other's ears, attacking blades of grass and otherwise behaving like a pair of

FACING PAGE: *A female coyote
plays with her month-old pups.
Pups are born in early May, leave
the den in June and remain with
their mother until the fall.*
W. PERRY CONWAY

puppies on a warm summer day. Every now and then one of them would leap up and nip at Mama's snout and she would look down briefly, but otherwise she rarely took her eyes off me or her third pup.

My first thought upon seeing these adult western coyotes in their natural habitat was that I was being granted a rare privilege, a glimpse into the private life of a very beautiful and intelligent species. I feel this way whenever I come upon life in the wild, whether watching a bull moose munching its way through the shallow end of a remote lake in northern Ontario or an otter performing its aquatic acrobatics in a fast-moving river in Algonquin Park. But coyotes are shy animals, and such encounters are infrequent and momentary.

The coyotes I had seen before had all been eastern coyotes, which are somewhat bigger and more ruggedly built than this western subspecies. Eastern coyotes are roughly the size and shape of German shepherds, and catching a glimpse of them in the forest does not produce that sharp intake of breath, that sense of the delicacy of nature, that these western coyotes produced in me. These animals were small and finely featured, more like large foxes than dogs, almost more feline than canine, with large ears and narrow snouts, and a bright pellage of variegated browns, black and off-whites that shone in the bright July sunlight with health and even pride. Here was none of that slinking, skulking behaviour so often attributed to coyotes: these animals were perfectly attuned to their environment, intensely alert and confident in their ability to fend for themselves. Let a river otter know you are watching it, or startle a bull moose in mid-browse, and it will disappear in a blind panic: the mother coyote in the wolf-willow meadow was well aware that I was watching her; she merely watched me back, playing absently with her two pups as she waited for me to move on, looking at me as if to say, "Okay, you caught us. Have a good look, because in a few minutes we'll be gone."

An adult eastern coyote pads along hard-packed snow in central Massachusetts. Eastern coyotes are bigger than western coyotes and are thought to have more wolf DNA. *They did not appear east of the Mississippi until the 1940s, moving down into New England from Canada.* BILL BYRNE

A coyote mated pair in eastern Colorado. Coyote social structure is extremely important, relying on strong family bonds and shared territories. W. PERRY CONWAY

Coyotes are so secretive that seeing one is a relatively rare occurrence, even though they are without a doubt the most numerous and successful large predator in North America. They are also the most widely distributed, having extended their range in the past hundred years to cover almost the entire continent, from Central America to Alaska, and from California and British Columbia to Nova Scotia and New England.

The coyote was known as God's dog by the Navajo of the American Southwest, where it probably originated, and as the medicine wolf by the more northerly Native peoples when it spread to the grasslands. Early European explorers called it the burrowing dog; to later settlers it was (and still is in the East) the brush wolf. Such a variety of local names is a reflection of its wide distribution as well as of its infinite variability: there is a world of difference between the image conjured up by "burrowing dog" and that suggested by "brush wolf," but both seem to fit the coyote perfectly.

To scientists, the coyote is *Canis latrans*, the name bestowed upon it in 1823 by Thomas Say, the naturalist who accompanied Major Stephen H. Long's ill-fated Great Plains Expedition to find the source of the Red River (they sailed up the wrong river by mistake). Say correctly identified *Canis latrans* as a North American member of the Canidae family and thus related to the grey wolf (*Canis lupus*), the red wolf (*Canis rufus*), the grey fox (*Urocyon cinereoargenteus*), the swift fox (*Vulpes velox*), the red fox (*Vulpes vulpes)* and, less remotely than one might think, the domestic dog (*Canis familiaris*). More distantly, the coyote is a relative of the golden jackal (*Canis aureus*) and the Cape hunting dog (*Lycaon pictus*). The Latin name means "barking dog," because Say noticed that coyotes, unlike wolves, made barking or yipping noises. Wolves howl on occasion, but coyotes vocalize at one another as a matter of daily communication.

Although it had long been assumed that coyotes originally descended from wolves, recent archaelogical finds and DNA analyses have determined that it is actually the other way around: coyote anatomy is more "primitive" than that of the wolf, and fossilized coyote bones from the Pleistocene, found in digs in Maryland and New Brunswick, predate those of the modern grey wolf by many thousands of years. All canids (and all felines) are descended from a tree-climbing, nail-retracting Pliocene mammal family known as miacids, which flourished more than 2 million years ago. When the miacids split into their various cladistic lines, coyotes seem to have remained in the south (the oldest coyote remains have been found in New Mexico), and the wolves appear to have migrated north, eventually crossing a Beringian land bridge into Asia. In their absence, coyotes spread to fill their niche; at some point, however, wolves returned to North America via a more recent land bridge—at about the same time that bison, bears and camels came to this continent—and

Coyotes prefer travelling along established trails, including human-made ones. Their track pattern is straight, with the hind paws registering directly on the prints made by the forepaws. JIM BRANDENBURG/MINDEN PICTURES

coyotes were pushed back into their historic range in the Southwest.

By the time Say encountered coyotes near Council Bluffs, Iowa, at the beginning of the nineteenth century, their range was pretty much confined to the Great Plains—what Long and others erroneously referred to as the Great Interior Desert between the Rocky Mountains and the Mississippi River—and from southern Alberta to central Mexico. Largely as a result of human activity since that time—the extermination of the wolf in much of central and northern North America, the creation of more and more grassland habitats where mice, voles and hares thrive, and the introduction of domestic livestock as an alternative food source— the coyote has again expanded its range into nearly every corner of the continent. It is now found in Alaska, British Columbia, Alberta and Saskatchewan and as far south as Costa Rica and Panama; since the 1920s, it has migrated east, probably moving north of Lake Superior into Ontario and Québec, down into New Hampshire and Massachusetts, back up into Maine and the Maritime provinces in the 1970s and 1980s. Wildlife biologist Adrian Forsyth estimates that there are now more coyotes in any given area of North America than there are red foxes.

Taxonomists have divided coyotes into nineteen subspecies (with the eastern coyote a possible twentieth), from the diminutive plains coyote (*Canis latrans latrans*), which weighs in at about 7 kilograms (15 pounds), to the larger mountain coyote (*Canis latrans lestis*), which can reach up to 20.5 kilograms (about 45 pounds). One spectacular eastern coyote in Maine weighed 31 kilograms (68 pounds). Because of their incredible adaptability—they have been said to rival rats and humans in their ability to survive under just about any conditions—they have become the most intensely studied predator in North America. They are also one of the most maligned and least understood of the continent's top predators.

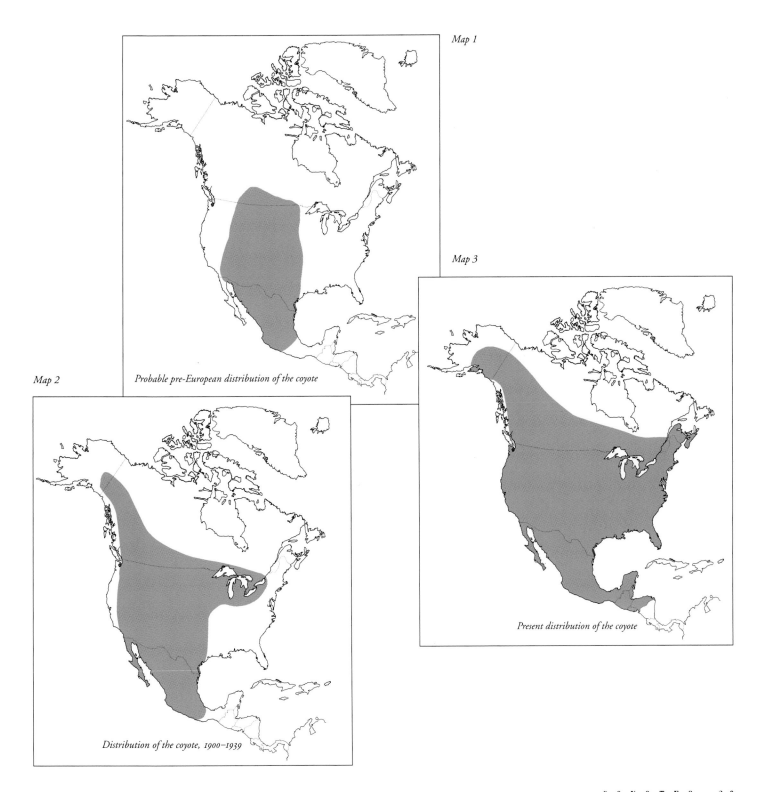

Map 1

Probable pre-European distribution of the coyote

Map 2

Distribution of the coyote, 1900–1939

Map 3

Present distribution of the coyote

*A coyote pack consists of a
dominant, or alpha, pair and one
or more associate family members,
depending on the availability of
food.* TOM & PAT LEESON

THE PACK

A coyote pack consists of three to eight animals, with an average of around six. The nucleus of the pack is the mating pair, also known as the alpha pair; these are the two dominant animals of the pack. There are also two or more associate or beta coyotes, younger adults whose main role is to defend the pack's territory and to help look after the pups and the nursing mother. Under normal pack situations, only the alpha pair breeds, so only the alpha female bears pups. Beta females do not even mate unless the coyote population is severely threatened, in which case the beta female will sometimes bear pups in the same den and at the same time as the alpha female. This phenomenon, however, is rare in natural

A pack's home range is around 15 square kilometres (5.8 square miles), slightly larger in winter.
TOM & PAT LEESON

The track of an eastern coyote's forepaw. Coyote tracks are oval, can be up to 6.5 centimetres (2.5 inches) wide by 9 centimetres (3.5 inches) long, with the claw marks of the middle toes close together. The tracks of the hind paws are smaller, and the heel pad is usually less prominently visible.
BILL FOURNIER

circumstances: in eight years of observing dozens of western coyote packs in unexploited environments in Washington and Wyoming, Bob Crabtree has seen it happen only twice. In the east, where coyotes often come into closer contact with human beings, and where pack structure is less common (in some places there are only mating pairs, with no beta animals at all), all females go into estrus, sometimes even during their first year. But in general, only the alpha female bears young. A litter usually consists of six to eight pups, although the range is from four to—in at least one recorded instance—twelve.

The associate or beta members are always siblings, the offspring of the alpha pair from a previous year's litter; thus, all pack members are also family members. Beta members are usually permanent; they are defined as juveniles who have not dispersed from the home pack by the end of November, when they are eight months old. Dispersed coyotes either become nomads (and there are some permanent nomads) or solitary residents or meet up with other dispersed coyotes of the opposite sex to become resident mating pairs and eventually alpha pairs of their own packs. Thus, an individual coyote can be classified in each of the different categories at various stages of its life.

The coyote is such an adaptive and widely dispersed animal, however, that it is very difficult to find a single place where this "average behaviour" is observed. Local populations respond to local conditions—food sources, terrain, exploitation by predators—making nonsense of definitive statements. As already mentioned, in areas where contact with human beings is more common, or where food is scarcer, as in some of the territories occupied by eastern coyotes, coyotes may not form packs at all but may live as mated pairs and raise pups that disperse when they are one year old.

The purpose of forming (or not forming) a pack may be to ensure the successful rearing of pups. The size of a pack is affected by the availability of food: a large pack requires more food, but it can also more effectively defend carcasses and territories, and so in areas where food is abundant, packs tend to be larger. Nature seems to have built a natural population control into the coyote's life cycle by making its period of gestation and birth coincide with the greatest scarcity of food: the end of winter and early spring, when rodents have not yet come out of hibernation, and ungulate carrion is least likely to occur. Ironically, humankind has altered that control mechanism in the coyote's favour by introducing alternative food sources at exactly that time of the year.

THE DEN

"The word 'den,'" writes Frank Dobie in his wonderfully anecdotal book *The Voice of the Coyote* (1949), "carries with it a popular misconception." This misconception is reflected in the ancient and inaccurate epithet "burrowing dog": coyotes do not live year-round in burrows as, say, prairie dogs or gophers do. Most of the time, coyotes sleep on open ground, in day beds, or "lays," which they form by turning around a few dozen times to press down tall grass or snow (the origin of that curious behaviour often seen in domestic dogs before they settle down on one's favourite chair). Even during denning season, just before and after the pups are born, only the female actually enters the den, generally just to nurse the pups. Other adults in the pack will bring food to the nursing mother, and later to the weaned pups, but very seldom do adult coyotes engage in any activity that could be described as burrowing, unless they are digging a ground squirrel out of its hole.

Dens are usually dug by the female, often with help from her mate, where the digging is easy: into sandy hillsides or stream banks, under rocky outcrops or fallen logs. Often coyotes merely renovate and enlarge badger or fox dens. Kezha Hatier, a coyote researcher who has studied coyote denning behaviour in the Lamar Valley in Yellowstone National Park, says that dens are usually 1 to 2 metres (about 3 to 6 feet) below the surface, and can extend well into a hillside, sometimes as deep as 8 metres (26 feet): "The tunnel opens into a larger chamber," she says, "and there is sometimes a second entrance, much better concealed than the main entrance. The main hole will have piles of dirt around it and be quite conspicuous, but I've seen coyotes scoot into secondary entrances that were almost invisible, as if they were diving right into the earth."

Good dens are re-used from year to year. A good den is one that is well hidden and easily defended, has a southern exposure so that pups and mothers can catch early spring sunshine, and does not flood during spring runoff.

Many researchers talk about the difficulty of finding a coyote den when coyotes are actually using it. Hope Ryden was one of the lucky ones, but until she found a den to study in preparation for her book *God's Dog*, she spent weeks in futile search. "Thousands of ground-squirrel burrows honeycombed the earth," she writes, "beckoning me to investigate them. But what actual coyote dens I found had vacancy signs hanging out front, in the form of cobwebs spun across their entrances." When she consulted with Yellowstone and Grand Teton park rangers, she learned that none of them had ever stumbled across an active coyote den. The day I spent with Kezha Hatier in Yellowstone's Lamar Valley, we found two abandoned dens on a steep, east-facing rock slide sheltered by a stand of pines, while Kezha's radio receiver told us that the mated pair we were tracking was somewhere on the other side of the valley. We never did find their den.

PAGES 34–35: *A litter of eastern coyote pups at the mouth of their den. Pups depend on food brought by pack members until they learn to hunt for themselves.* BILL FOURNIER

ABOVE: *Coyote dens are usually dug in sandy soil amid tree roots and can extend many metres into the ground.* TOM & PAT LEESON

FACING PAGE: *Pups stay close to the opening of the den during the day and are called back by the mother at feeding time or if she senses an intruder.* TOM & PAT LEESON

Coyotes keep track of territorial borders by leaving scent markings on prominent objects, such as this one on a frozen lake in Massachusetts. BILL BYRNE

To understand the role of the den site, it is important to know something about coyote territoriality. The entire area patrolled by a pack is its home range: depending on such factors as population density and the availability of food, a pack's home range can be as small as a few square kilometres or as large as 100 square kilometres (or about 40 square miles). The average home range in the mountains of Alberta, for example, is 12 square kilometres (4.6 square miles); in Arizona, it is around 55 square kilometres (just over 21 square miles). Similar spreads have been reported in eastern North America, from 16 square kilometres (6.2 square miles) in Vermont and Québec to more than 45 square kilometres (17.5 square miles) in Maine. There is some expanding and contracting of home ranges from season to season; a study in Grand Teton National Park in Wyoming found that a pack's home range widened from 24.6 square kilometres (9.5 square miles) in the fall to 60.5 square kilometres (23.4 square miles) in the winter, probably because in winter, when ground squirrels—coyotes' main food source in that region—are hibernating, coyotes have to search farther afield to find food. By comparison, wolf-pack ranges in northern Alberta have been measured at 250 square kilometres (nearly 100 square miles) in the summer, and 503 square kilometres (or almost 200 square miles) in winter. In general, a wolf's home range is about twelve times larger than that of a coyote.

Home ranges for smaller social groups are bigger than those of packs; Bob Crabtree, working in Washington in 1988, measured range sizes of 14.5 square kilometres (5.6 square miles) for social group members, 54 square kilometres (21 square miles) for solitary residents (who establish their own home range after leaving their home pack) and 220 square kilometres (85 square miles) for nomads. Studies of eastern coyotes in Maine have shown that social units rarely include more than two adults, and home ranges are usually twice as large as the average for coyotes in their historic range west of the Mississippi.

A coyote mating pair or coyote pack frequents the outer area of the home range but does not usually defend it. When a strange or migrant coyote wanders into the outermost area of another coyote's home range, it may be allowed to do so undisturbed, as long as it wanders out again fairly promptly. If it begins to hunt, feed on the home coyote's cached elk carcass, or otherwise behave as though it were thinking of moving in, there may be some perfunctory snarling and teeth baring, and the intruder will usually get the message and amble nonchalantly back into the nearest neutral zone. The outer area of home ranges can be thought of as a sort of buffer between rival packs, where minor transgressions are tolerated as long as they remain minor.

Within the home range is an area that is defended, though not strenuously, known as the pack's territory. A coyote that wanders into a pack's territory will be watched and perhaps even escorted out again. The territory comprises the pack's regular hunting area, and a pack will patrol it daily (or, to be more accurate, nightly). A pack knows the topography of its territory intimately: even young pups have an uncanny sense of where the best hiding places are, where all the trails go and what animals travel them, and where the prey hangs out. A territory will contain areas where carrion occurs fairly frequently—from wolf kills, road kills, hunter kills or some other non-coyote-caused fatality—as well as good hunting areas for smaller game such as ground squirrels and hares.

At the heart of the territory lies the pack's core area, a much smaller, much more intensely guarded zone in which coyotes spend most of their time—in one study, members of a radio-collared pack spent 80 per cent of their time in their core area, which comprised only about 7 per cent of the pack's total home range. Core areas have what are known as biological attraction points, such as good food sources, sleeping spots, protection from predators and a variety of good denning sites, because coyotes like to move from den to den after the pups are born. Core areas may also have other benefits, such as good views of surrounding areas, perhaps south-facing exposures. Massachussets wildlife tracker Paul Rezendes told me that he once came upon a coyote lay site in winter, a small area about the size of a living room containing eight lays; it was on the south side of a gentle slope overlooking a river valley, and the first thing that struck him was that from this shelf not only could the coyotes see everything that went on in the valley, but, because of the upward lift of the land, they could also hear everything even before they could see it. This is significant in light of the findings of coyote researchers Marc Bekoff and Michael Wells that when coyotes are hunting, "the senses that facilitate the location of prey are, in decreasing order of their importance, sight, hearing and smell." If Paul had looked around this coyote living room, he probably would have found a den site within close visual range.

Coyotes will defend their core areas from other coyotes and will defend their territories vociferously during mating and denning season—so vociferously that most coyotes will not cross territorial borders during these times. Even transients learn to give occupied territories wide berth from February to July, picking their way around the peripheries, through so-called corridors between home ranges, on their way to establishing home ranges of their own somewhere else. This business of avoiding confrontational situations by staying out of clearly defined territorial boundaries is an important evolutionary strategy for many species. Fiercely territorial birds like the mockingbird or the red-winged blackbird, for instance, have distinct call-signs that warn other members of their species that this particular spot is already occupied and will be defended if necessary. Intruders almost always respect the warning and fly somewhere else, thus saving everyone a lot of much-needed energy.

*Scent marking is performed in a
number of ways. The raised-leg
position, shown here, is usually
associated with males, although
females use it too when marking
objects above the ground.*
TOM WALKER

Coyote scat is never more than 2.5 centimetres (1 inch) in diameter and is usually composed of deer, rabbit or rodent hair and small bone fragments. It is almost always found in the middle of trails, especially where two trails cross. BILL FOURNIER

COYOTE COMMUNICATION

Coyotes have developed an intricate system of nonvocal communication, shared with other canines and felines, called scent marking, which is familiar to any pet owner who has ever tried to drag a dog past a telephone pole or get a tomcat off a porch. Domestic dogs scent-mark more or less out of species memory, since the idea of actually demarcating specific home ranges, territories and core areas in a city, and even attempting to defend them from the hundreds of other dogs living within forbidden proximity, would be not only ludicrous but probably dangerous to the dog's mental health. I have often wondered what a Doberman thinks when it sniffs the mark of a Chihuahua on one of its own scent-posts. Rural dogs seem less numbed to their instinct and bark mindlessly at the mere sight of another predator—a category that includes humans—within their territory. To coyotes, scent marking is not just a way to of keeping tabs on the neighbours; it is an intricate and crucial method of keeping peace among predators who have learned over the millennia that avoidance is a lot more conducive to evolutionary success than confrontation is.

Coyotes have two anal musk glands, one on either side of the sphincter, that secrete a strong-smelling pasty liquid that acts as a kind of personal identification for individual coyotes and, by extension, for packs. Every time a coyote urinates or defecates, it leaves its scent.

There are several kinds of scent marking, or "chemical communication," as researchers euphemistically call it. Virtually all elimination is a form of scent marking in the wild, because sooner or later some animal is going to detect and possibly interpret it. But matter deposited specifically as a message to other coyotes differs from simple elimination in several respects. A coyote is scent-marking when (1) it sniffs first and then marks, (2) it scratches the ground after marking, not before, (3) it directs urine on an object that it has marked before or that another coyote has marked before, and (4) it deposits only a small amount of urine at a time on a sequence of objects along a trail.

Generally speaking, males scent-mark by raising one of their hind legs, females by going into a semi-squat position and juveniles (and some females) by leaning slightly forward with the hind legs stretched straight back—though all three positions are adopted by males and females about 10 per cent of the time. Marc Bekoff, studying coyotes in Grand Teton National Park, noticed that coyotes tended to use the raised-leg method most often between November and April, suggesting that it is associated with courtship and mating; they used the squat method most from April to May, possibly in relation to pup rearing. The raised-leg method is more effective for marking objects that are off the ground—such as shrubs, stumps and rocks—from which scent is more likely to be picked up by other coyotes during

The squat method of scent marking is usually performed by females and is often associated with food-related activities such as hunting and marking carrion.

KATHY L. WATKINS/IMAGES
OF NATURE

winter, when a snowfall could cover up a scent deposited on the ground. Because territoriality is much more important during courtship and mating season than at other times of the year, it is in an individual's interest to mark its territory most clearly during that time.

Bekoff also noted that the squat method of scent marking seemed more often associated with food-related activities such as hunting, eating and marking carrion than with territoriality. A scent mark at the entrance to a trail leading to a kill site would be deposited in this manner, for example, and Bekoff hypothesized that it "may serve some type of bookkeeping function, indicating that food is no longer available at a specific site although food odours may persist." At any rate, scent marking by the raised-leg method is associated with males and courtship, and scent marking by the squat method is associated with females, pup rearing and food.

Coyotes communicate in other ways besides their scent. One of the most important is vocalization. Philip Lehner, in his paper "Coyote Communication," has identified eleven forms of vocalization, including the woof, the growl, the huff, the bark, the bark-howl, the yelp, two kinds of whine, something called the "wow-oo-wow" (a form of greeting), the group yip-howl and the simple group howl. All of these expressions signify different kinds of communication, from warning other coyotes away from a particularly tasty piece of food (the growl) to welcoming pack members into the core area (the woof), but even Lehner laments the "paucity of information" about coyote vocabulary. More study, as they say, is required.

FACING PAGE: *Researchers have identified eleven forms of vocal communication in coyotes, ranging from a simple greeting to the familiar howl.* TOM & PAT LEESON

The howl is used to keep pack members in vocal communication with one another. MICHAEL H. FRANCIS

Barking is often associated with territoriality, especially when accompanied, as here, by foot scratching. TOM & PAT LEESON

Sometimes coyotes howl for the
sheer joy of self-expression—in the
words of one researcher, giving
voice to "some deeper feelings and
needs of the caller."
DON ZIPPERT

COURTSHIP AND MATING

Among domestic dogs, mating is often a relatively impersonal affair involving no long-term commitment from the participants and no shared parental care if the mating succeeds in producing pups. This is understandable in domestic situations, in which the dog chow is guaranteed and the role of helping out with the pups is usually taken over by the female's human benefactors. Among wild canines, however, ensuring that the pups and the female are well fed during denning season means that the male has to stay around and help out with the chores.

Some observers believe that coyotes attempt to mate for life, although this is difficult to prove in the wild and behaviour in captivity is not always a reliable reflection of natural arrangements. But it is certainly true that the male-female bond is the most significant social unit among coyotes, more important even than pack social structure, which obviously depends on the bond between the alpha couple for its cohesion and effectiveness.

Females choose their mates very carefully, sometimes even indicating their preferences as pups; observers have noted six-month-old pups forming bonds that develop into lifetime partnerships. More usually, little sexual preference is shown until the second year—although females are capable of breeding at ten months, they usually do not breed until they are at least twenty-two months old; males, thirty-six. After that, females are infertile for ten months of the year, and males are sterile for eight months.

Courtship takes place during the late winter, when the serious business of choosing a mate (and thus passing two individuals' genetic codes on to future generations) begins in earnest. In mid-December, a female may have half a dozen male suitors from which to choose, all of them showing their interest, making themselves available, displaying their talents. The males remain at a respectful distance from her, following her about, sometimes for weeks. There is no vicious competition among them; they do not fight or growl at one another. They simply attend her pleasure. The female remains haughtily aloof during this time. Gradually, a few of the males lose interest and drift away, leaving only those rivals who are really interested, until finally only one or two are left.

Near the end of January, the female will finally accept one of the males, and the two will engage in an almost ritualized celebration of their bond. The female will go down on the ground and wriggle playfully back and forth under the male's chin, often reaching up to lick his muzzle, or to nudge his chest with her raised haunches. The male will stand and accept this tribute. And then there takes place what can only be described as a coyote love duet, a synchronized howling that tells any other coyote still in the area that a bond has been established. Hope Ryden observed this remarkable phenomenon in Yellowstone's Lamar Valley:

FACING PAGE: *A mated pair, the female, on the left, nipping playfully at the ear of her mate. Coyotes attempt to mate for life, and the success of the species depends on shared responsibility and mutual support.* RICK McINTYRE

A courtship chase across a frozen lake in central Massachusetts. The male will follow the female for weeks before she finally determines that he has the characteristics necessary to help her rear a family.
BILL BYRNE

At eight weeks (in late June),
coyote pups make short forays from
the den but are still largely
dependent on other pack members
for food and protection.
MICHAEL H. FRANCIS

PUPS

The gestation period for coyotes is sixty-three days, so the pups are born in April or the first week in May at the latest. They are altricial, which means they are born blind and helpless: their eyes open about ten days after birth, and the pups remain dependent on their mother for about fourteen weeks. During this time, the mother remains in more or less constant contact with them—Hope Ryden, watching a coyote den in National Elk Refuge, saw the mother leave her three youngsters in one den at regular intervals and go off into a clump of trees but later found that the mother was actually going to nurse three more pups that she had, for reasons of her own, sequestered in a second den.

While the alpha female is busy caring for her pups, the other members of the pack care for her. They bring her food, babysit the pups when she does go off on jaunts of her own and help her move the pups from one den to another. A core area will frequently have several den sites, and pups can be moved as often as every day, but they are usually moved less often. The mated pair that Kezha Hatier observed in Yellowstone moved its pups about ten times in three months. Pups will be moved for a number of reasons—for safety, of course, if the den has been discovered by a potential enemy, but also to avoid parasites that infest dens, such as fleas, lice, ticks and worms.

For the first week of the pups' lives, the mother rarely leaves the den; after that, she begins making forays for food and exercise, and will return to the den only to nurse the litter. At three weeks, the pups leave the den, at first tentatively, but after a day or two they will return to it only in alarm or to sleep. They cut their teeth at six weeks, at which time the parents will begin to introduce them to solids, both in the form of whole mice or voles and as regurgitated food: the adults gorge themselves on carrion and then return to the den to regurgitate part of their semi-digested meal for the pups. Pups encourage regurgitation exactly as vampire bats do, by nipping at the adult's lips. In fact, pups will continue to nip at an adult's mouth long after they have learned to eat nonregurgitated food. A habit so closely allied with survival must be a hard one to break. In Banff, I watched a pair of pups playing with their mother in early July, and much of their play consisted of leaping up and nipping at the corner of the mother's mouth while she sat quietly, tolerantly alert.

These first two months of pup rearing are the focal point of the coyote's year. The long winter is over, the pain and deprivation of parturition is past, and food and sunlight are once again plentiful. "For the mother," writes François Leydet in *The Coyote*, "this is a brief interlude of rest and tranquillity, which enables her to gather the strength she will need during the demanding weeks of the pups' education." Adults gradually increase the size of the food they bring back to the den, from field mice to ground squirrels to pocket gophers to rabbits, and from dead animals to living ones, so that the pups learn not only what to eat

ABOVE: *Coyote littermates are subject to a host of natural threats, including rattlesnakes and disease; usually only two survive into the fall.* WOLFGANG BAYER PRODUCTIONS

FACING PAGE: *A two-month-old coyote pup in Montana practises his group howl.* ALAN & SANDY CAREY

The entire pack contributes to the rearing of pups; older members bring food, take over babysitting duties and help in the education of their younger siblings. AUBREY LANG

Pups nip at their mother's mouth, inducing her to regurgitate semi-digested food, until they are old enough to hunt their own food.
ALAN & SANDY CAREY

Field mice, deer mice and voles make up the bulk of coyotes' summer diet, but they will eat almost anything in season, from fresh fruit to lizards. W. PERRY CONWAY

but how to kill it. Before long the pups are accompanying their parents and helpers, the pups' older brothers and sisters, on hunting excursions, at which time they learn not only to seek out carrion but also to watch for predators.

In unexploited populations, two pups seem to be all that survive into September, no matter how large the litter. Young pups are prone to a number of more or less natural fatalities, starvation being chief among them. They also succumb to diseases, to which starvation makes them more susceptible: canine distemper, often caught from domestic dogs; various other viruses transmitted through feces and the saliva of regurgitating adults; rabies (although rabies is very rare among coyotes); canine hepatitis. Eagles and owls will carry off unwary pups, as will bobcats, lynxes, mountain lions, wolves and wolverines: two of the four pups that François Leydet observed in Arizona in 1974 were killed by natural enemies, one by a bald eagle and another by a rattlesnake.

In the fall, the social organization of the pack undergoes a kind of shuffling, as it is decided which of the two pups will disperse to become a nomad, which will stay to become a helper and which of the previous helpers will disperse to set up packs of their own. There is no way of knowing how these decisions are made. The age of the alpha pair is a factor, as are the availability of food, the natural inclination of the pups and juveniles, and the nearness of unclaimed territory. But by and large, by the end of November the makeup of next year's pack is established; by mid-December the courtship rituals will have begun, and the entire cycle will repeat itself again as if for the first time.

PAGES 66–67: *Coyotes in southern Alberta subsist largely on snowshoe hares and carrion left out by sheep and cattle ranchers.* WAYNE LYNCH

PAGE 68: *In winter, carrion can make up nearly 80 per cent of a coyote's diet.* TOM & PAT LEESON

COYOTES & US

fresh salmon from some fishermen, he turned himself into a cedar plate; every time the fishermen placed a fish on the plate, the fish disappeared.

In real life, coyote the animal was every bit as complex and opportunistic as Coyote the Trickster was in the legends. The duality of the omnipotent hero with human foibles is reflected in that of the wild predator that wanders into camp begging for scraps. Both could be respected as well as befriended, summing up the Native relationship with nature in general. The Trickster's ability to change into whatever form suited the occasion was mirrored in the coyote's seemingly infinite adaptability to whatever environment it found itself in, from the deserts of New Mexico to Alaska's North Slope, from the mountains of Guatemala to the forests of New England.

By the beginning of the nineteenth century, the coyote was living more or less in harmonious proximity to human beings, with a relationship to civilization similar to that of foxes in Europe. Some aboriginal tribes had even domesticated the coyote, which they found somewhat more tractable than the wolf. Thomas Say noted in 1819 that the coyote was "probably the original of the domestic dog so common in the villages of the Indians," and the naturalist J. K. Lord later identified the dog of the Spokans as being "beyond all question nothing more than a tamed Coyote." Plains Indians had domesticated coyotes before they had horses and used them as beasts of burden to pull their travois and as sources of wool and food. Simon Fraser, who in 1808 explored the western half of the continent to the mouth of the river named for him, several times noted in his journal that the Salish people of the Thompson River regarded their dogs as highly useful members of society: "They gave us two excellent dogs which made delicious meals for the men, besides fish and berries in abundance. Here we procured a few articles of curiosity; viz., a blanket of Dog's hair, a matted bag, a wooden comb of curious construction, &c." The dogs were shorn, and their hair, mixed with that of the mountain goat, was woven on looms into blankets and rugs. "They made rugs of Dogs' hair," writes Fraser, "that have stripes of different colours crossing at right angles resembling at a distance Highland plaids."

Diamond Jenness, author of the classic *Indians of Canada*, shows how esteemed the dog was among the Assiniboines when he describes their principal religious festival, the sundance: "The ceremonies lasted three days. On the first the people danced; on the second the medicine-men displayed their conjuring tricks; and on the last the whole camp banqueted, giving dog's flesh a prominent place among the meats." Given the prominent place accorded the coyote in their mythology, it is not hard to believe that the dog of the Assiniboine was nothing less than the obliging, if somewhat domesticated, coyote.

THE OUTBREAK OF HOSTILITIES

It is hard to pinpoint exactly when the first shot was fired in the war against the coyote. The Spanish seem to have taken a dislike to the animal almost at first sight. The earliest European account of the coyote is found in a Latin text, *Nova Plantarum, Animalium et Mineralium Mexicanorum Historia*, published by Francisco Hernández in 1651. Hernández describes the *coyotl* as having "a wolf-like head, lively large pale eyes, small sharp ears, a long, dark, and not very thick muzzle, sinewy legs with thick crooked nails, and a very thick tail. Its bite is harmful." He then leaves natural history behind to delve into hearsay:

> It is said to attack and kill not only sheep and similar animals but also stags and sometimes even men. . . . It is a persevering revenger of injuries and, remembering prey once snatched from it, if it recognizes the thief days afterward it will give chase. Sometimes it will even attack a pack of its own breed and if possible bite and kill them.

A later reference, in the *History of Mexico*, written in 1780 by Francisco Javier Clavijero, is less damaging to the coyote's image: "*Coyotl*," wrote Clavijero, "is one of the most common quadrupeds of Mexico, in form like the dog, voracious like the lobo, astute like the fox, in some qualities resembling the jackal."

When Lewis and Clark made their foray to the West in 1804, they travelled almost to the foothills of the Rockies before encountering coyotes, or "burrowing dogs," as they called this new (to them) animal. Merriwether Lewis, in his journal entry for 5 May 1805, also called it "the small wolf," and noted that it was

> of intermediate size between the fox and dog, very delicately formed, fleet and active. The ears are large, erect and pointed; the head is long and pointed, like that of the fox; the tail long and bushy; the hair and fur are of a pale reddish-brown color, though much coarser than that of the fox; the eye is of a deep sea-green color, small and piercing; the talons are rather longer than those of the wolf of the Atlantic States, which animal, as far as we can perceive, is not to be found on this side of the Platte. These wolves usually associate in bands of ten or twelve, and are rarely if ever seen alone, not being able singly to attack a deer or antelope. They live and rear their young in burrows, which they fix near some pass or spot much frequented by game, and sally out in a body against any animal which they think they can overpower; but on the slighest alarm retreat to their burrows making a noise exactly like that of a small dog.

The war entered its official phase towards the middle of the nineteenth century, when ranchers began raising livestock on the American and Canadian prairies; coyote eradication

PAGES 78–79: *Coyotes in the West have been blamed for widespread sheep predation, although research suggests that few coyotes prey on livestock.* MICHAEL H. FRANCIS

FACING PAGE: *The eastern coyote has been linked to declines in deer populations. Recent evidence shows that deer herds are actually improved when predators cull old and sick animals.* BILL FOURNIER

programs coincided with the systematic elimination of *all* rivals for western range land, including bison, wolves, grizzlies and North American aboriginal peoples. When Mark Twain published *Roughing It*, an account of his sojourn in the American West from 1861 to 1867 as secretary to the territory of Nevada, he had little fear of being controversial when he described the coyote as a beleaguered but deserving victim:

> Along about an hour after breakfast we saw the first prairie-dog villages, the first antelope, and the first wolf. If I remember rightly, this latter was the regular coyote (pronounced ky-*o*-te) of the farther deserts. And if it was, he was not a pretty creature or respectable either, for I got well acquainted with his race afterward, and can speak with confidence. The coyote is a long, slim, sick and sorry-looking skeleton, with a gray wolf-skin stretched over it, a tolerably bushy tail that forever sags down with a despairing expression of forsakenness and misery, a furtive and evil eye, and a long, sharp face with slightly lifted up and exposed teeth. He has a general slinking expression all over. The coyote is a living, breathing allegory of Want. He is always hungry. He is always poor, out of luck and friendless. The meanest creatures despise him, and even the fleas would desert him for a velocipede. He is so spiritless and cowardly that even while his exposed teeth are pretending a threat, the rest of his face is apologizing for it. And he is so homely!—so scrawny, and ribby, and coarse-haired, and pitiful. . . .

Twain's description is typical of what had already become a full-scale campaign of coyote character assassination. Nothing he said would compel readers to defend the coyote if they then picked up a newspaper and learned that the coyote's "race" was being systematically exterminated, which, by the middle of the nineteenth century, it was. Cowboys shot every varmint they came across and carried sacks of strychnine in their saddlebags with which to inject every animal carcass they encountered—be it Texas longhorn, plains bison or Uinta ground squirrel—with the intention of killing any scavenging predator that fed on it. They were responsible for hundreds of thousands of coyote deaths; they also killed any other animal that fed on the carcasses or on the dead coyotes. Paul Paquet, a wildlife biologist now studying wolves in Banff National Park, Alberta, has documented twenty-eight different species of animals feeding on a single moose carcass in northern Manitoba, including wolves, bears, foxes, weasels, ravens, vultures, crows and domestic dogs: a dose of strychnine would have wiped out all of them.

Cattlemen eliminated the buffalo—60 million of them in a few decades—and introduced domestic cattle, which, it turned out, could not eat the natural prairie sweet grass that had nourished the buffalo. The cattlemen then imported European grasses to feed their European livestock. Areas that were too arid or too rocky or too remote for cattle grazing or railroad building or homesteading were given back to the federal government to become public domains—today, in ten western states, these public lands add up to more than half a million square kilometres (about 200,000 square miles). Most of these public domains, which were also natural coyote habitat, were taken over by woolgrowers, who promptly petitioned the federal government for permission to eliminate from their grazing lands any animal that might interfere with the profitable raising of sheep. In 1896, the Department of Agriculture obligingly set up a branch agency to deal with this emergency, the Division of Biological Survey—actually the new name for the old Section of Economic Ornithology, which had been established in 1885 to eliminate songbirds from grain fields, but that's another story. Although the principal target of the new division was the wolf, that hapless animal was extirpated by 1915, leaving a bureaucracy in need of a target, and the coyote was the only large predator left. As Hope Ryden puts it:

> Having no animal to extirpate might have proved embarrassing to the Biological Survey. . . had it not been for the existence of the coyote. Heretofore ignored, the coyote's occasional depredations now became a matter of overriding concern, and additional funds were obtained to eradicate him. So a new bureaucracy was born.

By 1922, the new bureaucracy included nine predatory animal inspectors in thirteen western states, the Control Methods Laboratory in Denver, Colorado, and $125,000 with which to pay local hunters to kill wild predators. François Leydet, in his book *The Coyote: Defiant Songdog of the West*, quotes a 1923 "Hunters' News Letter" from the division's Arizona office, in which two district hunters were chastized for "showing a no catch record" in December. "If the animals are in your district to be gotten," exhorted the inspector, "we feel that you should get them, and I do not feel that it is necessary for any man to work any length of time without catching some predatory animals." Four men were placed on the Honor Roll for having killed nineteen coyotes, eleven bobcats, two mountain lions and two wild dogs. "REMEMBER OUR SLOGAN," the letter ends: "BRING THEM IN REGARDLESS OF HOW."

The hunters took the division at its word: between 1915 and 1947, according to Frank Dobie, writing in 1949, "constantly expanding federally controlled operations, which include co-operation with states and with owners of live-stock, accounted for the destruction of 1,884,897 coyotes." This was an extremely conservative estimate, because it took no account of animals killed by ranchers and sheepmen and not reported, or of animals that were shot or poisoned and not retrieved. Most commentators double the federal figures. Nor did the killing stop in 1947: Hope Ryden quotes figures published by the Department of the Interior (to which the Biological Survey, renamed Predator and Rodent Control, or PARC, was transferred in 1939) showing that in a single year in the 1960s, government trappers killed 89,653 coyotes. Although there have been some name changes in the past fifty

FACING PAGE: *Since the late nineteenth century, millions of coyotes have been killed by trappers, hunters and ranchers.*

TOM & PAT LEESON

years—PARC was renamed Wildlife Services in the 1960s, then Animal Damage Control (ADC), and has now gone back to Wildlife Services—the war against the coyote is far from over. In 1992 alone, ADC "biological science technicians" killed 97,966 coyotes, nearly twice as many as all other "nuisance animals" combined, except songbirds.

Once the voice of the untamed American desert, the coyote is now one of the most persecuted of predators. RICK McINTYRE

Leg-hold traps and poisons have
been used to exterminate the
coyote from farm and range land.
MICHAEL H. FRANCIS

HOW TO KILL A COYOTE

The "how" of coyote control is a compendium of increasingly effective and inhumane methods. The early government hunters, known as *los coyoteros* in Mexico, or simply as federal coyote men farther north, used rifles and steel leg-hold traps—simple devices that snap two metal jaws together when an animal steps on a trip-release mechanism between the jaws. Although the unpadded leg-hold has come under fire in recent years as an inhumane method of trapping any animal, for most of this century it has been the main weapon in the hunter's arsenal. A study conducted in Alberta in 1990 found that injuries to coyotes caught in unpadded leg-hold traps ranged from small lacerations and muscle damage to compound fractures, separation of elbow and hock joints, freezing and gangrene, and actual limb amputation—the last occurring in two of the eighty-two coyotes included in the study. One coyote, the report states drily, "caught at the mid-carpal area, escaped with the trap on its foot. It was sighted 12 days later with the trap still attached. At this time, the coyote appeared to be thin and moved slowly. After another 10 days, it was seen with the trap and the trapped foot missing."

Later hunters, like Charles Cadieux, author of *Coyotes: Predators and Survivors*, who worked for the ADC in the 1960s, shot coyotes from airplanes and helicopters, which were owned by sheep ranchers and operated by the Department of the Interior. Or else they tracked the coyotes to their dens and fished out their pups with hooked wires: "After an hour of hard digging," Cadieux writes, "we were able to cable out seven pups by using a piece of telephone guy-wire with the ends unraveled and bent back to form hooks. An expert with this tool could tangle it in the hide of any coyote and pull him, protesting, to his fate." Cadieux also writes about tossing cyanide gas canisters into dens, igniting them and then covering up the den openings, causing the pups to die "quickly and almost painlessly." Less meticulous hunters poured gasoline into the dens, followed by a lighted match. Edward Hoagland, who spent some time with a coyote hunter when writing his essay "Lament for the Red Wolf," says that "compared to trapping, den-hunting is downright purist and arcane. It's catching the animals alive, by hand, in their hidden home, and some predator hunters hardly bother to trap at all, killing a presentable quota of coyotes just by finding and digging up the year's new dens." Hoagland's hunter knew enough about coyote mentality to know how to find the den: he would let the adult coyote spot him, so that "he will have the benefit of its last quick anxious glance in the direction of the den to guide him on," before he shot it.

The so-called Humane Coyote-Getter, or cyanide gun, was approved for government use in 1939. Also called a go-getter, it consisted of a 15-centimetre (6-inch) hollow aluminum tube that was driven into the ground; a spring mechanism was affixed to the top end, which

Many coyotes are killed each year for their thick pellage, which is mixed with wolf pelts for coats and parka trim. The slump in fur prices has inspired many trappers to call for a re-introduction of the bounty system. JOHN HENDRICKSON held a .38 calibre revolver case loaded with a small amount of gunpowder and sodium cyanide. Since coyotes cannot resist investigating any strange-smelling object within their range, the go-getter was baited with a tuft of sheep's wool smeared with an exotically scented lure—Frank Dobie says that the U.S. Fish and Wildlife Service recommended "a compound of rotten meat, especially horse, armadillo or prairie dog; rotten brains; a tincture of beaver castor; and . . . Siberian musk, which comes from between the toes of Siberian deer." When the coyote investigated the scent, pulling up on the wool with its teeth, it triggered the spring mechanism, which fired the gunpowder, which shot the cyanide up into the coyote's mouth and eyes. Death usually followed before the blinded coyote could run the length of a football field. The go-getter was used almost exclusively for many years, until ranchers began to complain that it was also killing their domestic dogs. "Every year there were dog losses," writes Cadieux. "This aroused much enmity for the coyote trapper." The device is still available, however, under the name M-44, and is still used extensively by sheep ranchers.

The predacide of choice in the 1940s was a wartime chemical known as sodium monofluoracetate, or Compound 1080, a poison so effective that only half a kilogram (1 pound) of it was enough to kill about 0.5 million kilograms (1 million pounds) of coyote: the normal dosage was 1.6 grams (½ ounce) of 1080 injected into 45.4 kilograms (100 pounds) of bait. "Compound 1080 does not produce a 'pretty' death," notes Cadieux. Working on the nervous system, it seems to speed up the metabolic processes so that the animal ages and dies in six to eight hours. "A 1080-killed coyote will end up lying on its side, all four feet going through very rapid running motions as it finally dies," Cadieux says. Another observer describes "a frenzy of howls and shrieks of pain, vomiting and retching as froth collects on his tightly drawn lips," and Cadieux calls 1080 "the most inhumane poison ever conceived by man."

Perhaps Cadieux had not heard of thallium, a tasteless, odourless metallic chemical that replaced 1080 in the 1960s. Thallium causes a slow, agonizing death, but only in 60 per cent of its victims; the rest just go blind and lose all their hair, and their toenails and teeth drop out.

All use of poison on public lands in the United States was outlawed by the Nixon administration in 1972, and the following year the Senate passed the Environmental Protection Act, which provided further solace to the beleaguered coyote. It is still legal to hunt coyotes on private land with traps, guns and dogs, however. In Ontario, legislation is being drawn up that will examine the entire question of coyote hunting—one plan is to limit the season to two weeks of the year, as is now the case with deer and partridge hunting, and to impose a bag limit. But elsewhere in Canada coyotes are fair game. According to Arlen Todd of the Alberta Department of the Environment, during the 1980s, when coyote pelts fetched sixty to one hundred dollars in the fur industry, about forty thousand coyotes were killed each year in that province. Today, with the collapse of the fur market, accurate figures are hard to come by, since fewer hunters are registering their kills. Similarly, in Ontario, Mike Buss of the Ministry of Natural Resources says that nearly forty thousand coyotes have been registered by hunters and trappers in the province over the past ten years, but he won't even hazard a guess as to how many actual coyote deaths that figure represents. Trappers have to register their kills only if they plan to sell the pelts, and with pelt prices so low in recent years, most don't bother.

Finally, a word should be said about inadvertent coyote hunting, which in some areas accounts for more coyote deaths than the intentional eradication programs undertaken by farmers. In Banff National Park, for example, according to park biologist Mike Gibeau, more coyotes are killed by automobiles and trains than by natural causes. Out of the eleven radio-collared coyotes in his two-year study of coyote-human interaction in the park, seven were killed by motorists. He calls the twinned highway between Canmore and the Banff townsite Death Valley for coyotes and is opposed to the park's plan to extend the double highway to Lake Louise. Coyotes hunting ground squirrels in the tall grass between the highway's fences are regularly picked off by cars. Distemper and canine parvo, brought into the park by tourists' domestic dogs, are also responsible for a significant rise in coyote pup mortality. "I figure up to 90 per cent of all the coyote deaths in the park are directly caused by humans," says Gibeau. "This is the opposite of what you'd expect a park to be. Normally," he says, "you'd expect a park to be dispersing animals out to an area where there is hunting. But we're not dispersing anything. Instead, we're a black hole; animals come here and are killed."

Despite more than a century of human predation, however, the coyote not only has expanded its range geographically but has also increased its numbers exponentially. As a result, there are more coyotes living in more places than ever before. Adolph Murie's classic study, *Ecology of the Coyote in Yellowstone*, published in 1940, tells a typical story. From 1907 to 1935, when coyote hunting was banned in the park, a total of 4,352 coyotes were trapped and killed, and yet Murie estimated that in 1935 there were more coyotes in the park than there had been at the turn of the century. Most scientists estimate that as many as 75 per cent of all coyotes in a population can be killed annually without causing an overall decline in numbers. It's like the old stories of the Trickster: the more Coyote is persecuted and even killed, the more he comes back in different and more elusive forms.

Coyotes have adapted well to human incursion. Caught stealing a free meal, this one displays submissive behaviour to its curious domestic cousin. MICHAEL H. FRANCIS

Highways are one of the coyote's chief enemies. In Banff National Park, Alberta, more coyotes are killed by cars than die from natural causes. JOHN W. WARDEN

Why have coyotes been so determinedly hunted? The simple answers—because they kill domestic livestock and because they kill game animals such as deer and antelope—do not stand up to even the cursory scrutiny they are sometimes given. There are, as described in Part 3, more effective and less costly ways to protect farm animals from predation than by trying to turn the entire continent into a sterilized breeding compound for herbivores.

Coyotes have inherited the reputation of the timber wolf, to a large extent. By an unfortunate accident of history, North America was colonized in the sixteenth century, when the fear of wolves was at its peak in Europe. Europeans brought to North America an attitude towards wolves that is pretty much summed up in such folk tales as "Peter and the Wolf" and "Little Red Riding Hood," stories in which wolves are cunning and malicious stalkers of innocent lambs and children. The behaviour of the velociraptors, about which scientists know almost nothing, in Steven Speilberg's *Jurassic Park* is extrapolated from the imagined ferocity of wolves as depicted in such works of fiction as Jack London's (and now Walt Disney's) *White Fang*. There is a superficial resemblance between the European tales of werewolves, for example—human beings that turn into wolves and kill other human beings—and Native American tales of "skinwalkers," human beings who turn themselves into coyotes and wreak havoc on their enemies. But the differences are instructive: a werewolf is a satanic creature; a skinwalker is a holy man, a man who turns himself into a god.

Barry Lopez, in *Of Wolves and Men*, attributes this hatred of wolves and coyotes to what he calls theriophobia, or "fear of the beast as an irrational, violent, insatiable creature. Fear of the projected beast in oneself." This is a much more generalized fear than the fear of wolves, because it extends to all wild creatures—to all of nature itself. In the five centuries since Columbus, we have systematically tried to wipe out every species that has interfered with what we consider to be our God-given right to exercise dominion over wild as well as domestic animals, over beasts of the forest as well as beasts of the field. In 1931, for example, the U.S. Senate passed legislation calling for "the destruction of all mountain lions, wolves, coyotes, bobcats, prairie dogs, gophers, ground squirrels, jackrabbits and other animals injurious to agriculture, horticulture, forestry, husbandry, game or domestic animals, or that carried disease." The Senate envisioned a North America inhabited by no other animal but livestock and game, nothing but what was controlled by or useful to human beings. Such legislation goes far beyond anything that can be called agricultural management or even predator control. It belongs to the category of revenge.

Coyotes have been chased on snowmobiles and in airplanes and helicopters until they drop dead from exhaustion or heart failure. Their carcasses have been hung on fences as "a warning to other coyotes." Rattlesnakes have been dropped into dens full of pups. In *The*

Carson Factor, an account of a disastrous coyote eradication program in Klamath County, Oregon, in the 1930s, William Ashworth writes:

> Otherwise decent men, men fond of their wives and children and tenderly solicitous toward dogs, horses and sheep, have been known to gleefully wire captured coyotes' mouths shut and turn them loose to starve, or to saw off their lower jaws with hacksaws, or to bind gunnysacks around them, douse it with kerosene, and set it afire, or to purposely leave them in traps for up to a week after they have been captured, waiting for their wounds to putrefy and their bodies to dehydrate, making sure that they suffer before they die.

Hope Ryden, describing the public outcry that finally was heard when some of the more inventive methods employed by federal coyote hunters came to light, quotes a letter from Dr. Raymond F. Bock of the Pima Medical Society in Arizona to the U.S. Department of the Interior: "One wonders," wrote Dr. Bock, "whether someone in your department has gone mad from a personal hatred of predators. . . . We wonder what kind of misfits may be perpetrating this campaign."

But the ultimate revenge may still be the Trickster's. Jeremy Schmidt, who lives in Jackson, Wyoming, tells a story about a local rancher who caught a coyote that he suspected had been killing his sheep. Rather than kill the coyote outright, the rancher tied a stick of dynamite to it, lit the dynamite and let the coyote go.

Coyote ran straight under the rancher's brand new pickup truck and lay down.

FACING PAGE: *A coyote carcass hung on a farmer's fence in Oregon. In 1992 alone, Animal Damage Control agents killed 97,966 coyotes in the United States.* THOMAS KITCHIN

Despite attempts at eradication, the coyote has extended its range from such areas as the Mojave Desert, shown here, into most of North America. JEFF FOOTT

PAGE 100: *Coyotes now exist in such disparate places as Alaska, New England and Montana, where these two coyotes were photographed.* ALAN & SANDY CAREY

PART 3

COYOTES & COMMON SENSE

COYOTES & COMMON SENSE

Through all these new, imaginative, and creative
approaches to the problem of sharing our earth
with other creatures there runs a constant
theme, the awareness that we are dealing with life. . . .

—Rachel Carson, *Silent Spring,* 1962

CAUGHT IN THE CROSSFIRE

Ontario's Bruce Peninsula is a rocky point of second-growth forest and hard-won farmland that juts out into Lake Huron to form the western shore of Georgian Bay. It comprises the province's two main sheep-producing counties and in recent years has been the focus of a fierce battle over predator control—read coyote hunting. Hunting coyotes here is a traditional winter sport. Sheep farmers with nothing much else to do from November to May park their pickups along concession and side roads and pick off coyotes with their .303s, often without even getting out of their cabs. Some of them are paid by the municipality to do it; others just do it for fun. Coyotes, they all say, are killing sheep, and the only way to prevent famine in the land is to kill coyotes. The sheep industry in Ontario, like everywhere else on the continent, is not a healthy one, and coyotes, many sheep farmers believe, are to blame for it.

Coyote predation on sheep has become a kind of rural myth. In Grey and Bruce counties, about 250 sheep, or 1 per cent of the 25,000 sheep raised on the peninsula, are report-

PAGES 102-103: *A coyote pounces on a vole.* TOM & PAT LEESON

FACING PAGE: *Coyotes are one of the few natural enemies of porcupines, although as the quill in the nose of this coyote in Banff National Park attests, voles are much safer prey.* THOMAS KITCHIN

COYOTES AND SHEEP

In the Trickster stories, Coyote is often and even easily killed. In one, he is shot with a magic arrow by Chickadee, who also kills Elk with a flint knife and three wolves by tossing them elk meat wrapped around red-hot rocks. But Coyote, and only Coyote, keeps coming back to life. Elk does not recover from predation, and neither does Wolf. This is as true in nature as it is in mythology. As Donald Worster notes in *Nature's Economy*, "ancient Indian myth says 'brother coyote' will be the last animal alive on earth, and in fact he has already outlasted many of his primeval associates."

The more coyotes that are killed by hunters, trappers and farmers, the more they seem to spring back in even greater numbers. Coyotes are not an endangered or even a threatened species, and hunting them is legal almost anywhere in North America. Although bounties and poison have been outlawed, the coyote is officially defined as a nuisance animal, a furbearer or a game species in most states and provinces: hunting coyotes for sport is as legal and as traditional as hunting deer or ducks, and there are no specified seasons or bag limits for coyotes, as there are for all other game animals. In the state of Kansas, the coyote is one of the few animals that can legally be shot from a vehicle. Even hunting coyotes with specially trained hounds is permitted and is as common in many parts of North America as fox hunting was in England in the nineteenth century. But the coyote is doing just fine, thank you, despite a century and a half of "controls." Perhaps it is time to re-examine our approach to establishing some kind of harmony between coyotes and us.

Except in an extremely localized sense, coyote control does not work; in the long run, leaving coyotes alone might be a more effective way of decreasing their numbers. In Yellowstone, Murie found that after coyote control was halted in 1935, the coyote population density declined naturally, and thus, by 1942, there were fewer coyotes in the park than when controls had been in place. The natural mortality rate for coyotes older than one year of age is from 35 to 40 per cent; when mortality rises, as it does when coyotes are subjected to predator-control programs, the coyote responds by increasing its litter size, raising the percentage of females that become sexually active in their first year and allowing beta females to breed. The result is more coyotes. Conversely, when left to their own devices, coyotes succumb to natural controls—starvation, disease, injuries such as infection from porcupine quills and predation by such animals as mountain lions, rattlesnakes, eagles, grizzlies and wolves. Even elk, normally a prey species, can be predacious when the opportunity arises. In Banff, Mike Gibeau named one of his radio-collared coyotes Lucky, because just as Mike came upon him while checking his trap site, he found a full-grown female elk about to kick the coyote's skull in. "If I hadn't come along when I did," says Mike, "that coyote would have been killed for sure." If all we wanted was fewer coyotes, not hunting them might be the best way to achieve that result. The outcome of all these more or less natural controls is a stable population.

The rationale for human intervention in coyote control is based on a misconception about the nature of coyotes. There is no denying that some coyotes kill old, sick and isolated sheep or cattle, lambs or calves, and a few healthy adults as well. As long ago as the 1930s, biologist Charles C. Sperry examined the stomach contents of 15,000 coyotes collected over a five-year period: his report showed that rabbits made up 33 per cent of the coyote's total diet; carrion was second at 25 per cent; rodents were about 18 per cent; and domestic livestock 13.5 per cent. Even at that, *The Cain Report on Predator Control* in 1970 estimated that the value of sheep and lambs lost to all predators in the twelve western states was $22.3 million, most of which was chalked up to coyotes. In 1978, the U.S. Fish and Wildlife Service calculated that coyote predation alone cost North American sheep farmers $19 million. The latest figures from the U.S. Department of Agriculture state that 500,000 sheep are lost to predation each year, 60 per cent of them to coyotes.

But there is also no doubt that coyotes do much less damage to livestock than is claimed by livestock owners. The Department of Agriculture gets its data from sheep ranchers and, as Donald Schueler pointed out in a profile of the ADC in a recent issue of *Sierra* magazine, such figures "are likely to be highly inflated." Many other animals besides coyotes prey on livestock; in fact, many other canines, including coyote-dog hybrids (coydogs), wolves, wild dogs and domestic dogs, kill livestock. But coyotes generally take the rap: investigations carried out in southwestern Ontario in 1992 found that about half of the 152 livestock attacks reported to the MNR as coyote kills the previous winter were probably the work of coydogs, and another 53 were carried out by domestic dogs running loose. Similar figures are reported wherever livestock compensation programs require official identification of the predating species: what farmers call coyote kills are quite often the work of other predators.

The reason for such misidentification may be that domestic dogs, coydogs and coyotes are practically indistinguishable from a distance. Biologists often have to resort to morphological evidence to define the difference between domestic dog and coyote skulls: they check the narrowness of the animal's snout and measure the ratio of the length of the upper tooth row (first premolar to last premolar) to the palatal width (the distance between the upper first molars). Animals with a ratio of more than 3:1 are usually coyotes; those with ratios of less than 2:7 are dogs. In some of their colour phases, coyotes even resemble wolves: the eastern coyote in Ontario, for example, is almost the same size and colour as the Algonquin wolf, largely because hybridization has caused them to share a lot of the same DNA. Pelts of both species are often thrown in together at fur auctions, making exact records of trapping figures difficult to maintain.

There may also be a more economic explanation: compensation for lost livestock is paid

A coydog, foreground, is a cross between a coyote and a domestic dog. Coyotes are often blamed for damage caused by these hybrid look-alikes. LEONARD LEE RUE III

to farmers out of municipal budgets if a domestic dog does the killing and out of provincial funds if the culprit is a wild animal such as a coyote. Since the inspection of claims is carried out by municipal appointees, there could be a built-in bias towards wild-animal predation as the cause.

Nearly every investigation of reported high coyote predation on farm animals has exonerated the coyote. In British Columbia's Fraser Valley, where in the 1980s local farmers had complained that coyotes were killing their sheep in unconscionable numbers, a two-year study of coyote scat and stomach contents determined that small rodents constituted 70.2 per cent of coyotes' diet and rabbits 8.2 per cent. Most of the rest was made up of raccoon, opossum, muskrat, deer, plants and insects: only 0.2 per cent of coyotes' total diet was sheep, and that could easily be accounted for as carrion.

Sheep production in North America has more than halved in the past three decades as a result of various economic factors—rising production costs, the introduction of synthetic fibres to replace wool, the importation of cheaper meat from New Zealand, as well as increased predation by wild animals—but there is no solid basis for placing a significant amount of the blame on coyotes. Researchers unanimously agree with Marc Bekoff's 1979 study, in which he found little evidence that coyote predation was the primary factor in decreased sheep production: "Coyotes do kill sheep, as well as other livestock and poultry," Bekoff reported in *Scientific American*, adding that "many factors other than coyote predation can cause considerably heavier damage." Bekoff cites a study conducted in the early 1970s that showed that in Idaho, where $2.3 million in sheep losses had been reported in one year, 36 per cent was attributed to disease, 30 per cent to "unspecified causes" and 34 percent to predation: only 14.3 per cent of those losses could be traced to coyotes. Most sheep farmers curse disease, the high cost of feed and disobliging weather as much as they rail against predating coyotes, but, as one Bruce County farmer puts it, "coyotes are the only one we can do much about."

Even if coyotes were primarily responsible for the sheep farmers' woes, killing them is not an effective means of protecting flocks. In fact, it may have exactly the opposite effect— not only because coyote numbers tend to increase when the population is exploited but also because of the kind of coyotes that survive the control measures. Bob Crabtree argues that killing adult coyotes at certain times of the year could actually result in an increase in lamb predation. "When the pups are a few weeks old, in early to mid-May," he says, "they place enormous pressure on the adults in the pack to provide them with food, and that's when the adults just go out and get the fastest protein source they can find. In some areas, that will be spring lambs rather than mice. Now, what happens if you kill off some of those adults? You end up with fewer adults having to provide the same number of pups with fast meat. What will they do? They'll go out and kill more lambs."

Crabtree also believes that killing adult coyotes in the fall and winter—as is typically done, since that is when their pelts are prime and that is also when sheep farmers traditionally hunt—may actually increase their numbers in the spring and summer. "Reducing adult numbers," he says, "increases the food-to-adult ratio, which may induce the alpha female to have larger litters, better milk and so on."

In 1971, the United States reported spending $8 million annually for a program that killed roughly 40,000 coyotes (there are an estimated 300,000 coyotes in the state of Kansas alone). In Canada, millions of dollars are spent each year compensating farmers for coyote- and wolf-killed livestock (the 1992 budget for this program in Ontario alone was $700,000). Much of this money is spent unwisely. For example, an analysis of the cost of coyote control in Arizona in 1960 showed that the state spent $157,603 to kill 1,864 coyotes: that year, the list of livestock killed by coyotes—539 sheep, 375 poultry, 182 cattle, 41 pigs, 17 goats, 2 dogs, 1 cat and 2 horses—was valued at $42,225. More recent examples are even more graphic. Donald Schueler cites a case in New Mexico in which ADC agents spent almost 500 hours killing 56 wild animals, "including 28 coyotes, a deer, several skunks, badgers, porcupines and foxes—plus a hognosed snake—all in response to a rancher's claim that a coyote had killed one lamb worth $83."

Might not some of that money be better spent helping farmers to improve their flock management by taking the coyote's life cycle and feeding habits into consideration? Knowing that coyote activity peaks twice each year, for example—in May and June, when pups are most demanding, and again in late August, when groundhogs decline and adult coyotes are teaching their four-month-old pups to hunt—could suggest to farmers that keeping a closer watch on their flocks during those periods would be a good idea. Similarly, knowing that coyotes will be most likely to attack livestock when other food sources are scarce, farmers could follow the peak and crash cycle of other prey species, such as hares. In eastern Ontario, for example, the snowshoe hare population peaked in the winter of 1992 and crashed the following summer—and that summer sheep farmers complained of record numbers of coyote attacks on their livestock.

Some of that money might also go into research into improving health measures for sheep. Sheep are notoriously susceptible to a staggering range of natural afflictions, from birth defects and mastitis to parasites and tuberculosis. As Hope Ryden notes, "a common saying among sheep ranchers themselves is that lambs come into the world 'trying to die.'"

Finally, the compensation programs for coyote- and wolf-killed livestock needs serious re-examination. Abuses seem almost to have been built into the legislation. As already noted, animals killed by domestic dogs are compensated by the municipality out of local tax money that might better be spent on roads; those killed by wild animals are paid for out of provincial coffers—and the inspectors are hired by the municipality. Farmers are not compensated for sheep that succumb to disease, but a dead sheep showing signs of coyote predation is compensable: the temptation to drag a diseased sheep out into a field for a night or two before reporting it missing must be all but irresistible. All of these practices artificially inflate the figures for sheep predation by coyotes and add to pressure on wildlife officers to solve the "coyote problem."

There are two devices on the market designed to protect sheep from coyotes, both developed in the ADC's research centre in Denver, Colorado. One is a siren-and-strobe scare device, called Electronic Guard, that emits a high-pitched wail and flashing light when triggered by an invading predator. The other is a propane cannon that works more or less the same way. Both devices have been used by ranchers with some success, although they undoubtedly scare the sheep even more than they do coyotes, and scared sheep produce fewer lambs.

Guard dogs—especially such Eurasian breeds as the Akbash—and even llamas have proven to be more effective in protecting sheep, and an experiment conducted in Ontario by Ministry of Natural Resources biologist Karen Bellamy also shows great promise. She raised a donkey with a flock of sheep and let the donkey graze with the flock in the summer of 1992. She found that the donkey, an animal as fiercely territorial as the coyote, protected the flock from predation as effectively as dogs, with less training, less feeding and less supervision. "You can only place one donkey in with the sheep," says MNR's Maria Delmeida, who followed the experiments, "because two donkeys will spend more time with each other than with the sheep. And one donkey can look after a flock of only about 150. But it was a very promising study nonetheless." A goat farmer I know placed a donkey with her goat herd and was pleased with the result, until she found that the donkey was straying off to join a field of horses nearby instead of watching her goats. Still, she lost only one goat to coyotes last year; it had got its head caught in a fence as it reached through to graze the greener grass on the other side.

There are even simpler ways to protect sheep than using dogs and donkeys. In Alberta, Arlen Todd found that one of the most effective ways of getting rid of coyotes is simply to dispose of livestock carrion in such a way that coyotes cannot get at it. Abandoned sheep and cattle carcasses are a major food source for coyotes. Another study by Todd found that farm carrion comprised more than 60 per cent of the diet of coyotes that lived in agricultural areas and 40 per cent of the diet of coyotes that lived in forested areas some distance from farms. These figures suggested to Todd that coyote distribution in some areas is actually determined by the availability of agricultural carrion. He wanted to know what the coyotes would do if farmers stopped leaving dead animals around for them to forage on. On most farms, when an animal dies of age or disease it is simply hauled out into a field or bush and left to rot—in Todd's two control townships near Westlock, Alberta, more than 6800 kilograms (15,000 pounds) of carrion was normally exposed in this way each winter. In 1973, Todd convinced farmers in two other townships to burn small carcasses (poultry and piglets) and to use dead-stock removal companies for larger carcasses, thus reducing the amount of carrion available to coyotes to about 680 kilograms (1,500 pounds). There was some initial opposition to Todd's experiment; farmers thought that without carrion either the coyotes would leave the area, causing an increase in rodents that would lead to an increase in crop damage, or else packs of "hunger-driven" coyotes would simply turn from feeding on dead stock to preying on livestock. Which of the two possibilities would actually happen was exactly what Todd wanted to find out.

He found that in areas where carrion was unavailable, the coyotes either increased their consumption of rodents or else moved to another area—usually the area in which carrion was still being left out. In December and January, both carrion-free townships showed a 93 per cent decline in coyote population, with a consequent decrease in livestock predation. Perhaps more significantly, there was no increase in livestock depredation in the two control townships, even though many of the coyotes leaving the experimental area went to the control area in search of carrion.

A coyote hunts voles on a frosty morning. Studies show that coyotes prefer low, rodent-rich valleys to high meadows, where bighorn sheep are plentiful. TOM & PAT LEESON

ABOVE: *Coyotes catch small prey like pocket gophers every 20 minutes.* MICHAEL S. QUINTON

FACING PAGE: *Coyotes successfully run down rodents about 60 per cent of the time.* W. PERRY CONWAY

Two coyotes pull down a white-tailed deer in mid-ford. Being smaller than wolves, coyotes use running water or deep snow to aid them in hunting. MICHAEL H. FRANCIS

Defending domestic livestock herds is not the only reason given for the war against coyotes. More than a few hunters admit that their aim is also to protect deer or other game populations from overpredation—the more coyotes they kill, in other words, the more deer will be available for them to kill as well.

This attitude is a holdover from earlier times. Adolph Murie noted in 1940 that predator control in the park began only "when hunting was so wanton as to imperil the existence of game animals," the object of coyote control being to eliminate "any factor which might be considered in any way inimical to the well-being of the game"—any factor, that is, except game hunting itself. There was absolutely no scientific support for the supposition that coyotes were depleting deer or elk populations in the park (or anywhere else). But from 1877 on, a fierce battle against all predators was waged in Yellowstone, and strychnine-laced carcasses led to the eradication of wolves, wolverines and mountain lions by the mid-1920s. Murie quotes the 1889 report by park superintendent F. A. Boutelle, which stated that "the carnivora of the park have, in common with other animals, increased until, I believe, something should be done for their extermination." As Murie notes sourly, the fact that game animals were increasing did not seem to incline park authorities to a reconsideration of their attitude towards predators. "In Superintendant Anderson's report for 1896," he writes, "coyote control is recommended because the animals were numerous, not because they were injurious."

The report by Superintendant George Woods for 1909 veers breathtakingly close to sentience: "Quite a number of coyotes were killed last year," Woods wrote, "about 60—but still they seem to increase. It is doubtful, however, if they kill much game, as the deer seem able to protect themselves. On several occasions last winter, I saw deer chasing coyotes instead of being chased by them." But still the war went on: in 1910, a total of 40 coyotes were killed in the park; in 1911, the total was 129; in 1912, it was 240. From 1907 to 1935, a grand total of 4,352 coyotes was expunged from the park, along with 132 grey wolves (the last one was killed in 1925) and 121 mountain lions.

Murie's study showed that Woods's speculation that coyotes do not feed much on deer was quite correct. From an analysis of coyote scat samples over several years, Murie determined that deer and elk constitued only 17.1 per cent of the coyotes' total diet, the bulk being composed of field mice (33.9 per cent) and pocket gophers (21.6 per cent). Snowshoe hares comprised 3.4 per cent, and grasshoppers 7.9 per cent. He also found that most of the deer and elk ingested by coyotes was in the form of carrion—animals that had died naturally of age or disease or starvation, not of coyote predation.

More recent studies have borne Murie's observations out. In Alberta, Arlen Todd studied the stomach contents of 542 coyotes trapped in the forested regions of that province between 1972 and 1975 and found that ungulates provided only 11 per cent of the coyotes' total diet. In contrast, up to 77 per cent consisted of snowshoe hare. In fact, Todd found that coyote populations fluctuated according to the abundance of hares, not ungulates. Murie had anticipated these findings in 1942, when in a study of wolves in Mount McKinley National Park he noticed that coyotes did not inhabit the upper ranges, where mountain sheep were plentiful, but preferred to remain in the lower valleys where "the staple rodent supply is more abundant."

Although some studies show that in parts of New England the eastern coyote may have a significant impact on white-tailed deer populations—especially in years when the number of deer is high and the number of snowshoe hares is low—the consensus is that ungulate predation by coyotes is not as significant in determining their numbers as are other factors, such as the amount of precipitation during the previous summer. "Throughout most of their range in [Ontario]," write the authors of the MNR report "Wolves and Coyotes in Ontario," "coyotes have caused relatively little damage either to wildlife or livestock, and on the balance sheet they should be classed as beneficial to the economy." In fact, the report says that "we have no authentic reports of coyotes attacking deer in this province." The report lists field mice as the coyote's principal food source, comprising nearly 30 per cent of its diet, followed by rabbits and hares (15 to 40 per cent), groundhogs (in summer, until the end of August) and just about anything else that is edible, "either vegetable or animal . . . ," including apples and even wheat.

Even in areas where coyotes are killing deer, killing coyotes may have no effect on the number of predations on deer. The Maine Department of Inland Fisheries and Wildlife (MDIFW) has recently rejected the reintroduction of bounties in that state to control coyote predation of deer, because, it said, "bounties are generally not effective in reducing predation, are subject to fraud, and . . . serve only to subsidize a small number of hunters with no increase in overall numbers of the prey species the bounty is intended to protect." As MDIFW biologist Henry Hilton points out, this is because "the fall coyote trap harvest is predominantly juvenile animals, and . . . the most damage-causing coyotes are dominant adults." In other words, the animals caught by bounty hunters would not be the same animals that were killing deer.

Perhaps the real question ought not to be whether top predators kill ungulates —of course they do—but rather whether ungulate herds are harmed by such predation. Under natural circumstances, over time, they are not. A study conducted in the Welder Wildlfe Refuge in southern Texas, for example, determined that more than 50 per cent of fawn mortality in white-tailed deer was attributable to coyote predation, and yet the deer herds continued to thrive. To test the effects of coyote predation, the researchers fenced off a 391-

hectare (966-acre) "exclosure" and removed the coyotes from within it so that the deer population inside was effectively unbothered by coyotes for five years. What they found is worth quoting in full:

> Deer densities within the exclosure . . . tripled compared to outside, remained stable for two to three years, and then declined precipitously to levels only slightly above those recorded outside the exclosure. Forage for deer within the exclosure deteriorated significantly. The general health of the deer declined noticeably and parasite loads increased. Ultimately, the decrease in early postnatal mortality was compensated by increased mortality among fawns six to twelve months of age. Coyotes clearly were affecting survival of young deer. The removal of fawns by coyotes at earlier ages apparently helped maintain the remaining herd in much better physical condition.

Murie found more or less the same thing in Yellowstone in 1940. He concluded that coyotes exerted a "negligible" effect on the park's elk population; after decades of virtually unchallenged predation, he reported, they had made "no appreciable inroads in the populations of deer, antelope and bighorn sheep." In fact, Murie suggested that deer herds may even be improved *mentally* by coyote predation: coyotes teach them wariness, which protects them from all predators.

Coyote predation on deer herds may actually be less damaging to the population than human hunting, since human hunters tend to take adults in their prime, thus culling the best of the herds rather than the worst, as coyotes and wolves do.

PAGES 126–127: *A coyote in Yellowstone National Park gives chase in winter. The coyote's large paws give it an advantage over elk in all but the deepest, softest snow.*
W. PERRY CONWAY

Whether defending an elk carcass from other coyotes in Yellowstone, above, or driving off marauding ravens in Montana, right, the ears-back, teeth-bared stance says, "Keep off." ABOVE: HENRY H. HOLDSWORTH; RIGHT: ALAN & SANDY CAREY

ABOVE: *Rolling in carrion is a popular canid pastime.* BILL BYRNE

PAGES 130–131: *Mountain sheep are not threatened by coyotes: Adolph Murie "found no evidence of coyote predation on the bighorn" in Yellowstone.* MICHAEL S. QUINTON

THE COYOTE'S ROLE IN NATURE

In the tales of the Shuswap of the Northwest Pacific Coast, Coyote created Klamath County, Oregon. In the beginning there was no land, only a single great lake. Coyote came along in a canoe, looked down into the water and saw Pocket Gopher's lodge, called Pocket Gopher up and asked his help in setting things right. Pocket Gopher opened his mouth and produced fish, roots and berries. Coyote created mountains and gave names to the mountain lion, the bear, the elk and the deer. Then he created smoke, a sure sign that he had also created people, and "the people increased rapidly, and the animals and plants on the mountains multiplied."

In the early 1940s, the citizens of Klamath County, Oregon, instituted an intensive campaign to eradicate the coyote from their farmlands. Over a period of a few years, and by a variety of methods, more than ten thousand coyotes were killed. By 1947, there was not a single coyote in Klamath County. But there were field mice: in the absence of any natural control, the rodent population exploded. In 1947, the field mouse population alone was estimated at 25,000 per hectare (10,000 per acre); the cost in lost crops soared into the millions of dollars, far more than had ever been attributed to damage by coyotes. The cost of exterminating the field mice was also high; the incident is known to history as the Mouse War. In the end, Klamath County began to reintroduce the coyote to its farmlands. The whole exercise, from coyote extirpation to mouse eradication to coyote reintroduction, was an object lesson in understanding the balance of nature before blundering in to tamper with it.

We still do not understand the role of every animal in the ecosystem. As Mike Gibeau puts it, "Nature is like a balloon; we know that if we squeeze one end of it, it's going to bulge out somewhere else. We just never know where." And yet we persist in the belief that we can control nature, that in fact nature requires our control to run efficiently and effectively. The coyote, like other predators, has come to be a symbol of this attitude. In *Nature's Economy*, Donald Worster notes that "the coyote has been the object of America's concentrated moralistic fervor, and his tenacious survival represents an outrageous defiance of man's righteous empire over nature."

Worster suggests that "in the twentieth century, the coyote, along with other varmints and predators, has come to be viewed in a radically different light by many Americans." In this new light, a world without predators is seen as "a world that is in trouble." This is true. Klamath County certainly saw it that way after it had gone through the Mouse War. In many areas today, the coyote is not as "cordially detested," as John Muir put it in 1872, "by nearly all cultured people." Pat Wolff, manager of a group of wildlife defenders in Santa Fe, New Mexico, called Forest Guardians, has been working for years to abolish such government-sponsored programs as that carried out by the ADC. "When I first learned about ADC's war on wildlife and saw photos of animals being tortured and killed," she says, "it outraged me that a federal agency should be slaughtering wildlife for the benefit of the ranchers—with taxpayers' money." Elsewhere, biologists and animal-rights defenders are working to educate the public about the beneficial role predators perform in keeping rodent populations down and ungulate herds healthy. We are beginning to appreciate the extent to which tampering with a single strand of nature alters the whole fabric.

But many of us still tend to regard nature as a kind of living museum; if we remove one exhibit, we feel, we will not harm the entire display. This has been reflected in our various national parks policies since the setting aside of Yellowstone and Banff in the 1870s, it has given rise to the idea of "good" animals and "bad" animals, and it is still very much a part of the way we think about nature today—witness the continued wolf eradication programs in Alaska and the Yukon, and the pressure being placed on the Ontario government to eradicate the coyote from Grey and Bruce counties. One of the first repercussions of the recent disclosure by geneticists that the red wolf, an endangered species, may in fact be a cross between wolves and coyotes was a petition from Texan ranchers to remove the red wolf from protection under the Environmental Protection Act because the EPA does not apply to hybrids, even though hybridization is a natural mechanism by which new species are created.

Nature is not a museum, it is an organic system, and the removal of any link in its unfathomable chain weakens the whole and impoverishes us all in ways we cannot know. Coyotes remind us of this simple truth. Our attempts to remove the coyote from our midst are a symbol of our arrogant assumption that we can control nature, bend it to our will, alter it in ways that are beneficial to us. The real consequences of that assumption are apparent today in the devastation we have wrought upon our environment. We need to progress from arrogance to wisdom. Perhaps by studying and appreciating the coyote's role in nature, we will learn much about our own place in it as well.

FOR FURTHER READING

NATURAL HISTORY

Ashworth, William. 1979. *The Carson Factor.* Cambridge, Mass.: Hawthorn Press.

Bekoff, Marc. 1978. *Coyotes: Biology, Behaviour and Management.* New York: Academic Press.

Boer, Arnold H., ed. 1983. *Ecology and Management of the Eastern Coyote.* Wildlife Research Unit, University of New Brunswick, Fredericton.

Cadieux, Charles L. 1983. *Coyotes: Predators & Survivors.* New York: Stone Wall Press.

Dobie, J. Frank. 1949. *The Voice of the Coyote.* Boston: Little, Brown and Company.

Hyde, Dayton O. 1990. *Don Coyote.* New York: Ballantine Books.

Kolenosky, George. 1974. *Wolves and Coyotes in Ontario.* Ontario Ministry of Natural Resources, Wildlife Branch, Toronto.

Leydet, François. 1977, 1988. *The Coyote: Defiant Songdog of the West.* Norman: University of Oklahoma Press.

Murie, Adolph. 1940. *Ecology of the Coyote in the Yellowstone.* United States Department of the Interior, National Parks Service, Washington, D.C.

Olsen, Jack. 1971. *Slaughter the Animals, Poison the Earth.* New York: Simon & Schuster.

Pringle, Laurence. 1977. *The Controversial Coyote: Predation, Politics and Ecology.* New York: Harcourt Brace Jovanovich.

FACING PAGE: *The coyote reminds us that the removal of any link in nature's chain weakens the whole and impoverishes us in ways we cannot know.* RICK McINTYRE

Ryden, Hope. 1975, 1979. *God's Dog: The North American Coyote.* New York: Lyons & Burford.

Van Wormer, Joe. 1964. *The World of the Coyote.* Philadelphia: Lippincott.

NATIVE LITERATURE

Lopez, Barry Holstun. 1977. *Giving Birth to Thunder, Sleeping with His Daughter: Coyote Builds North America.* New York: Avon Books.

Malotki, Ekkehart. 1985. *Gullible Coyote: A Bilingual Collection of Hopi Coyote Stories.* Tucson: University of Arizona Press.

Mourning Dove, 1933, 1990. *Coyote Stories.* Lincoln: University of Nebraska Press.

Ramsey, Jarold, ed. 1977. *Coyote Was Going There: Indian Literature of the Oregon Country.* Seattle: University of Washington Press.

INDEX